To God Be the Glory: On S.C. Death/Life Row

By James Nate Bryant III

*Edited by
Sherry B.
Dave D.*

To God Be the Glory: On S.C. Death/Life Row

Dedication

*This book is dedicated to
Mr. James N. Bryant, Jr. and
Mrs. Helen Marie Bryant.
May the Most High continually bless
Ms. Marianne Lyden and family
along with so many others I am
praying for.*

Permissions

Where indicated/noted scripture quotations are taken from the Holy Bible, New Living Translation, copyright ©1996, 2004, 2007, 2013, 2015 by Tyndale House Foundation. Used by permission of Tyndale House Publishers, Inc., Carol Stream, Illinois 60188. All rights reserved.

Where indicated/noted scripture taken from the New King James Version®. Copyright © 1982 by Thomas Nelson. Used by permission. All rights reserved.

Chapter One

Let us always give thanks to the Lord, for He is good! His faithful love endures forever. You're loved alright! You'd better believe it! For God says in John 3:16

"For God so loved the world that He gave His one and only Son, so that everyone who believes in Him will not perish but have eternal life."

I would often ponder if the police corporal I killed over 16 years ago has this eternal life. My horrific behavior that caused this son of the Most High to die is just as ugly as the sinful nature of those who crucified our Lord Jesus Christ nearly 2,000 years ago. In the same manner in which Jesus forgave those who crucified Him, saying "Father forgive them, for they don't know what they're doing." Luke 23:34 (NLT) I pray that the police corporal's widow forgives my ignorant self. God knows it all but I'm only speculating as I pray without ceasing.

The glory of God has a broad meaning but for years I've been writing, keeping daily accounts in my journals setting out to write the things that were most significant to me throughout the course of the day and how God got the glory out of it. It's certainly by His grace that I've done any good or prospered at all in what I set my hands to do. I've turned my life over to the One and only True God. I'm living for Him now, but this was not always so. I thought there was a right way, a wrong way and my way. Leaning on my own understanding eventually had to hit the highway! There is so much I'd like to say but only some of these thoughts are to be revealed, necessarily and hopefully in a kind manner.

I was first encouraged to write a book about the things in my life by Cousin Margaret Ford. My mother Helen Marie Bryant would let me stay over at their house in Brookesville, S.C.

when I was a boy. I loved spending time with her sons, who are both now gone from this world through tragedy. The strong encouragement she'd be giving them falls on my ears now and oh how blessed I am that she pointed me to write, get it done, so she can read it. Hallelujah!

Bringing shame to my own family, especially my parents was something I'd never thought to do. Not on this level anyhow. I've apologized to the victim's family, my own friends, family, and 3 beautiful daughters, Jamia, Tanisha and last but not least Braeden. I've lived apologetically and still don't even realize all the lives I brought pain to. My agenda is to bring healing to all I come in contact with now through letting Christ's love be the sole force of anything I'm saying or doing. The Lord and so many others know how often I get it wrong but I'm trying and discover daily that I am and can *continue to live a purposeful life driven by the same love that saved many from themselves and hell.*

Some consider South Carolina death row to be hell on earth to a degree, but that has not been my experience, nor has it been that of some others I've met here. Time after time, prison chaplains, volunteer prison ministers and visiting church members has expressed their renewed view of men incarcerated here after meeting them. Their preconceived notions went from thinking of us as depressed, hopeless, dark individuals in dire need of uplifting, hope and light; to a more actual perception of somewhat normal individuals, full of character and perseverance. Correctional officers usually learn after only working one or two days on the row that most of the men have an above average attitude as far as prisoners go. A handful of *times I've heard South Carolina Department of Corrections' staff say that working here on the row is preferred over working in other parts of this prison. Others have said that working on the row is one of the best kept secrets in the S.C.D.C. I was first sent here in July 2001 after my first capital punishment trial. I don't want to talk about <u>myself</u> but desire to put much emphasis on the **One** who allowed me to be alive to tell you about the **Glory** we have and give to*

God our Father. He is sovereign, all-wise, all-knowing and present all over the place. Yes, He's present here on what I call S.C. Life row!

I believe with all of my heart that my name is written in heaven in what is called the Lamb's Book of Life. I believe that Jesus wrote it there along with other names of those who have left this prison either by execution to death; or by getting their death sentence changed, which got them a lighter sentence. There were *some men here with me that died due to illness bodily and mentally. I'm believing that there will be more people in heaven than the ones we knew to live and die righteously.*

Can I get an Amen to that?

Can I?!

Chapter Two

What I never want to forget is that God deserves all the honor, glory, praise and thanksgiving. We learn as Christians to give God the glory for what He has done, is doing and promises to do. His words always come to pass. Jesus asked the Father to glorify His Son, so He could give the glory back to Him. I've asked our Father to do the same thing and now I'm giving the glory back to

Him through this book and whatever I write in it ought to bring Him glory; and by no means do I desire to make myself out to be anything other than what I've become through grace by faith in His Son Jesus. Having said all that, I'm recalling where I heard this word <u>glory.</u> As I grew from a youngin to an older youngin, I heard it spoken in the Lord's Prayer, which was taught to us by our elders (grandparents, parents, uncles, aunts, etc.). My family would often

pray what is commonly known as the Lord's Prayer, first found in the King James Bible in the book of Matthew, chapter six, in verses nine through thirteen. It starts with: <u>Our Father</u>' and ends with, "For thine is the kingdom, and the power, and the glory, forever. <u>Amen</u>."
Although I often use the word glory in different expressions I remember that we'd have no glory at all if it wasn't given to us foremost. Just like the breath in our bodies that

we have....it's written in Genesis 2:7 (KJV) that God our Creator breathed into his (mankind's) nostrils the breath of life and man became a living soul. This English word <u>glory</u> found in Matthew 6:13 (KJV) was translated from the Greek New Testament. Here is what I found in my Greek dictionary. The word used in this instance is doxa, (dox'ah) as very apparent (in a wide application- literally, or figuratively, objectively or subjectively) meaning *dignity, glory or glorious honor, praise or worship. The Webster's dictionary says that glory is very great praise, honor, or distinction bestowed by common consent; renown. Def. #2 says something that is a source of honor, fame or admiration; an object of pride. Def. #3 adoring, praise or worshipful thanksgiving. Def. #4 resplendent beauty or magnificence. Def. #5 a state of great splendor or prosperity. Def. #6 a state of absolute happiness,* gratification, etc. Def. #7 the splendor and bliss of heaven; heaven. Def. #8 to exult with triumph; rejoice proudly. And I do not want to leave out this interjection. Def. #9 <u>glory be</u>. Glory be to God (used to express surprise, elation etc.) and an Idiom. Def. #10 goes to (one's) glory, to die. Well there we have it!!! It's fitting that the first mention of the word glory in The Holy Bible is found in the book of Genesis. Let's go to the King James

Version of Genesis, chapter 31:1.
It reads:

"And he heard the words of Laban's sons, saying, Jacob hath taken away all that was our father's and that which was our father's hath he gotten all this glory."

We gain insight to glory's very specific meaning as it is expressed here in this verse of Scripture. Our evolving English language has put it this way in the New Living Translation of Genesis 31:1, saying,

"But Jacob soon learned that Laban's sons were grumbling about him. 'Jacob has robbed our father of everything!' they said. 'He has gained all his wealth at our father's expense.'"

The word glory and wealth mean the same thing in this instance. It would be an injustice if we did not look at the Hebrew definition of glory. Hebrew 3519, kawbowd, (kaw-bode`); rarely Kabod, (kaw-bode`); weight but only figuratively in a good sense, splendor or copiousness;

glorious(ly), glory, honour (-able).

Doesn't the saying, "throwing your weight around" shed light on what glory means here? Jacob's wealth is what these other men had a problem with. It was surely the same blessing of Abraham and Isaac that these sons of Laban gave witness to, albeit unknowingly, in Jacob's life. We can sum it up by simply saying "Glory be to the God of Abraham, Isaac and Jacob!

Chapter Three

There are over 300 uses of the word glory in the King James Bible! We are getting a sense of the vast usage and meaning. In this chapter we'll see places from God's word where angelic beings (seraphim), living creatures and elders are giving glory to God. Doesn't that sound like something we all should want to be doing? Can you believe it?

The prophet Isaiah wrote in 6:1-4 about these mighty seraphim, which are heavenly beings not mentioned elsewhere in Scripture by that name. These creatures are described as each having 6 wings, with 2 wings they covered their faces, with 2 they covered their feet, and with 2 they flew. They were calling out to each other, "Holy, holy, holy is the Lord of Heaven's Armies! The whole earth is filled with His glory!" Their voices shook the temple to its foundations, and the entire building was filled with smoke.

I like the way the New Living Translation puts this. It's so vivid!

I have to clearly speak about and convey what I have learned so far about this glory that is really, truly, actually and presently in the whole earth. It's acknowledged more so by believers and of those who do not necessarily have faith in the words found written in the Holy Bible. Although *most of what I am lead to write about is based on the Scriptures, I also speak from my own experiences while prayerfully hoping that I'll get to see many more years of God's glory here in the earth....and not die on S.C. Death/Life Row, where I'm learning to tell what the Lord of my life has done.*

King David penned a similar statement in Psalm 118:17, "I shall not die, but live and declare the words of the Lord."

Let's take a look at Psalm 19 (NLT) which is a psalm of David.

"1) The heavens proclaim the glory of God. The skies display his craftsmanship. 2) Day after day they continue to speak; night after night they make him known. 3) They speak without a sound or word; their voice is never heard. 4) Yet their message has gone throughout the earth, and their words to all the world. God has made a home in the heavens for the sun. 5) It bursts forth like a radiant bridegroom after his wedding. It rejoices like a great athlete eager to run a race. 6) The sun rises at one end of the heavens and follows its course to the other end. Nothing can hide from its heat. 7) The instructions of the Lord are perfect, reviving the soul. The decrees of the Lord are trustworthy, making wise the simple. 8) The commandments of the Lord are right, bringing joy to the heart. The commands of the Lord are clear, giving insight for living. 9) Reverence for the Lord is pure, lasting forever. The laws of the Lord are true; each one is fair. 10) They are more desirable than gold, even the finest gold. They are sweeter than honey, even honey dripping from the comb. 11) They are a warning to your servant, a great reward for those who obey them. 12) How can I know all the sins lurking in my heart? Cleanse me from these hidden faults. Keep your servant from deliberate sins! Don't let them control me. Then I will be free of guilt and innocent of great sin. 14)

May the words of my mouth and the meditation of my heart be pleasing to you, O Lord, my rock and my redeemer."

Wow! The psalmist sums it up neatly and you can see his admiration for the Creator of all that he sees and knows.
I came across a few men awhile back who do not believe that King David nor his son Solomon were real characters in the Bible stories. Do you have faith in these words? Do you believe that the words in this Psalm 19 are inspired

*by a reliable source? This is what the prophet Samuel had to say about David.
1 Samuel 13:14 (NLT),*
"But now your kingdom must end, for the Lord has sought out a man after His own heart. The Lord has already appointed him to be leader of His people, because you have not kept the Lord's command."

Samuel spoke these words to King Saul whom David replaced. The Lord later told Samuel this in 1 Samuel 16:1 where it says: Now the Lord said to Samuel,

"You have mourned long enough for Saul. I have rejected him as king of

Israel, so fill your flask with olive oil and go to Bethlehem. Find a man named Jesse who lives there, for I have selected one of his sons to be my king."

In addition, the book of Acts 13:22-23 says: But God removed Saul and replaced him with David, a man about whom God said "I have found David son of Jesse, a man after my own heart. He will do everything I want Him to do.' "And it is one of King David's descendants, Jesus, who is God's promised Saviour of Israel."

I'm saying exactly what King David wrote in Psalm 19:1. The heavens proclaim the glory of God. The skies declare His craftsmanship. Right now I live in a 14x6 ft prison cell in solitary confinement, but each month I get to see the moon go through each of its cycles. I spied a full moon just 2 nights ago! I see the sun and clouds as I peer out of the dual slender windows just 2 feet away from the desk I'm at. Glory be to God for the sunshine on my shoulders and face now that the clouds has moved out the way! I feel its warmth and who do you suppose I give the glory and *much thanks to for these things? Jesus.*

Chapter Four

I experience God's glory daily in one way or another. He's done so much for me already in my 45 years here on this earth. I praise Him daily and even recognize that He is the King of glory. Let's visit another psalm of David. Psalm 24:1

1 "The earth is the Lord's and everything in it. The world and all its people belong to Him.

2 For He laid the earth's foundation on the seas and built it on the ocean depths.
3 Who may climb the mountain of the Lord? Who may stand in His holy place?
4 Only those whose hands and hearts are pure, who do not worship idols and never tell lies.
5 They receive the Lord's blessing and have a right relationship with God their savior. 6 Such people may seek you and worship in your presence, O God of Jacob. *Interlude*
7 Open up, ancient gates! Open up, ancient doors, and let the King of glory enter.
8 Who is the King of glory? The Lord, strong and mighty; the Lord, invincible in battle.

9 Open up, ancient gates! Open up, ancient doors, and let the King of glory enter.
10 Who is the King of glory? The Lord of Heaven's Armies--He is the King of glory." *Interlude.*

Back when I was first sent to this place of earthly punishment, I acquired a Baptist Hymnal about 2 or 3 weeks later. That was in 2001. On the page before the very first song I found this verse of Scripture written as a prelude.

Colossian 3:16 which says: "Let the message about Christ, in all it's richness, fill your lives. Teach and counsel each other with all the wisdom He gives; Sing psalms and hymns and spiritual songs to God with thankful hearts."

I do what I can to share all the goodness, grace and mercy the Lord sends my way. I'm dedicated to fulfilling my purpose and experience what I know to be the joy of the Lord each day of my life. The very next verse of Colossians 3:17 give this strong encouragement:

"And whatever you do or say, do it as a representative of the Lord Jesus, giving thanks through him to God the Father."

Let's not only be hearers of God's word but let's do it with all of our hearts. That's what I'm learning to do and I realize that I have the peace of mind that I was searching for all of my life. James and Helen Bryant taught me, loved me and corrected me but I went astray from God's ways and their ways. **I'm back!** *I want to live the rest of my life obeying God's command to honor my* *father and my mother. This same King of glory promised this blessing of long life to those who obey Him. For it is written in Exodus 20:12*

"Honor your father and mother. Then you will live a long, full life in the land the Lord your God is giving you."

And Ephesians 6:1-3 has this to say:

1 "Children, obey your parents because you belong to the Lord, for this is the right thing to do."

2 "Honor your father and mother."
This is the first commandment with a promise.
3 If you honor your father and mother, "things will go well for you, and you will have a long life on the earth."

I have never had such a deep, deep, deep desire to live longer! Knowing that I am a prisoner with the state of S.C., wanting to execute me for my crimes, keeps the issue of my earthly existence in my forethoughts. I'm learning to trust that whatever plans God has for my life lines up with this Scripture verse from Jeremiah 29:11, that prison ministers, loved ones, family & friends, have given me to read and believe on nearly 100 times since I've been in prison.

Jeremiah 29:11 "For I know the plans I have for you," says the Lord. "They are plans for good and not for disaster, to give you a future and a hope."

I say "To God be the glory for whatever plans He has for this son!"

Chapter Five

I see God's glory in the forgiveness He offers to those who tell Him about their sins. I am so thankful that we can go to our Father for forgiveness of our sins. These following words in 1 John 1:8-10 (NLT) become understandable when we look to Him for our help:

8) "If we claim we have no sin, we are only fooling ourselves and not living in the truth. 9) But if we confess our sins to Him, He is faithful and just to forgive us our sins and to cleanse us from all

wickedness. 10) If we claim we have not sinned, we are calling God a liar and showing that His word has no place in our hearts."

While waiting for my trial which was set for June 2001, my mother had me read, study and meditate on more than a few essential Scriptures about forgiveness. In my lawless, sin-filled state, I cried out to God before I'd even been arrested and then convicted nearly a year later in court. Every person sins. God's Son Jesus was the only one who never did go against God's will. We have God's glory through forgiveness that only comes through faith in His blameless Son. Romans 8:27-30 (NLT) puts it in this way:

27) "And the Father who knows all hearts knows what the Spirit is saying, for the Spirit pleads for us believers in harmony with God's own will. 28) And we know that God causes everything to work together for the good of those who love God and are called according to His purpose for them. 29) For God knew His people in advance, and He chose them to become like His Son, so that His Son would be the firstborn among many brothers and sisters.

30) And having chosen them, He called them to come to Him. And having called them, He gave them right standing with Himself. And having given them right standing, He gave them His glory."

The New King James Bible puts it this way in verse 30:

"Moreover whom He predestined, these He also called; whom He called, these He also justified; and whom He justified, these He also glorified".

All believers are justified and glorified! God has given us His glory just as if we'd never sinned. Trusting in God each of us can boldly say "He loves me, just if I'd

<u>never sinned!</u>" Let the justified give glory to the One who loves us and gave His life for us. Hallelujah!

Chapter Six

Let our children see Your glory. I have the sneaking suspicion that someone asked in prayer that her children might see God's glory. I recall my mother mentioning different parts of Psalm 90 over recent years. This one is a prayer of Moses, the man of God. The final two verses of this psalm (90:16-17 NLT) says:

16) "Let us, your servants, see you work again; let our children see Your glory. 17) And may the Lord our God show us His approval and make our efforts successful. Yes, make

our efforts successful!"

Moses asked to see God's wondrous works and to let the children see God's glory. The word glory conveys the idea of weight, significance, and importance here. Moses had astoundingly requested even a greater sense of God's presence than up to then, had not been experienced by any person. Moses had already lead God's people out of the land of Egypt as recorded in the book of Exodus. As God was instructing him about going into the Promised Land,

Moses responded by asking God to show him His glorious presence. In Exodus 33:17-19 says:

17) "The Lord replied to Moses, "I will indeed do what you have asked, for I look favorably on you, and I know you by name. 18) Moses responded, "Then show me your glorious presence." 19) The Lord replied, " I will make all my goodness pass before you, and I will call out my name, Yahweh, before you. For I will show mercy to anyone I choose and I will show compassion to anyone I choose." *(Please read Exodus chapters 33 and 34 for more details.)*

The Lord of heaven and

earth immediately showed Moses His glory which is His goodness, according to Exodus 33:19; so we can agree that God's glory is also God's goodness. Asking to see God's glory is a very good thing and I cried out in my frustration not two months ago (summer 2016), that I might see His glory. Now I can hardly speak, sing or write without giving Him the glory, honor, praise and thanksgiving He truly deserves. I see His glory in His mercy towards me and *my daughters. I know I don't deserve it! I'm fully convinced that He's showing me and also giving me understanding of His glory. It's not because He loves me so much, but because He loves us and sent His Son Jesus to die for us all.*

I'm praying, "Let my own children see Your glory."

Chapter Seven

This same special, unique Son was tempted by the devil. We will see how the glory of kingdoms and the authority over them were being used by the accuser and adversary of the children of God. The book of James chapter 1:12-18 (NLT) has this to say about temptation and where it comes from:

12) "God blesses those who patiently endure testing and temptation. Afterward they will receive the crown of life that God has promised

to those who love Him. 13) And remember, when you are being tempted, do not say "God is tempting me." God is never tempted to do wrong, and He never tempts anyone else. 14) Temptation comes from our own desires, which entice us and drag us away. 15) These desires give birth to sinful actions. And when sin is allowed to grow, it gives birth to death. 16) So don't be misled, my dear brothers and sisters. 17) Whatever is good and perfect comes down to us from God our Father, who created all the lights in the heavens. He never changes or cast a shifting shadow. 18) He chose to give birth to us by giving us His true word. And we out of all creation became His prized possession."

Here is Luke's account of the temptation of Jesus in chapter 4:1-13:

1) "Then Jesus, full of the Holy Spirit, returned from the Jordan River. He was led by the Spirit in the wilderness, 2) where he was tempted by the devil for forty days. Jesus ate nothing all that time and became very hungry. 3) Then the devil said to him, "If you are the Son of God, tell this stone to become a loaf of bread." 4)But Jesus told him, "No! The Scriptures say, 'People do not live by bread alone.'" 5) Then the devil took him up and revealed to him all the kingdoms of the world in a moment of time. 6) "I will give you the glory of these kingdoms and

authority over them," the devil said, "because they are mine to give to anyone I please. 7) I will give it all to you if you will worship me." 8) Jesus replied, "The Scriptures say,' You must worship the LORD your God and serve only him.'" 9) Then the devil took him to Jerusalem, to the highest point of the Temple, and said, "If you are the Son of God, jump off! 10) For the Scriptures say, 'He will order his angels to protect and guard you. 11) And they will hold you up with their hands so you won't even hurt your foot on a stone.'" 12) Jesus responded, "The Scriptures also say, 'You must not test the LORD your God.'" 13) When the devil had finished tempting Jesus, he left him until the next opportunity came."

At that time Jesus knew He would be Ruler of the world. His time to be in authority over these kingdoms would certainly come but not by His submitting to the devil. The glory of these kingdoms was really what He desired but He waited on His Father. That's what we're going to have to do whenever the glory of the things we want presents themselves. 1 John 2:15-17 gives us clear instruction so that we won't give into temptation.

15) "Do not love this world nor the things it offers you, for when you love the world, you do not have the love of the Father in you. 16) For the world offers only a craving for physical pleasure, a craving for everything we see, and pride in our achievements and possessions. These are not from the Father, but are from this world. 17) And this world is fading away, along with everything that people crave. But anyone who does what pleases God will live forever."

There are certain things that each of us want in our lives. All the good things we desire in life have a specific glory, big or small. There will be things we'll have to wait for. Things that we really want...like a new house, car, job or even a spouse. It's best for us to be obedient to God and wait on His timing, guidance and provision. There is one thing that is worse than waiting on God; wishing that you would have! To God be the glory, for the great things He does for us! My hope is that we'll be able to say what David did in Psalm 27:13-14 (NLT).

13) "Yet I am confident I will see the Lord's goodness while I am here in the land of the living. 14) Wait

patiently for the Lord. Be brave and courageous. Yes, wait patiently for the Lord."

Chapter Eight

Glory... Isaiah 58:8 (NLT)

....."the glory of the Lord will protect you from behind."

This is my greatest personal lesson about the glory of the Lord; which is promised to those who fast the fast that the Lord has chosen. In Isaiah 58 God teaches about true and false worship, the kind of fasting that pleased God and the fasting that the hypocrite does. This chapter in our Holy Bibles starts out with a very clear and simple message that our nation , states, cities, communities and families need to hear, during these troubling times we're experiencing. God's glory is God's presence! As believers we are taught through Ephesians 6:10-18 to put on the whole armor of God. That armor is all frontal but we need God's glory to protect us from behind. Let's read Isaiah chapter 58 prayerfully:

"Shout with the voice of a trumpet blast. Shout aloud! Don't be timid. Tell my people Israel of their sins! 2) Yet they act so pious! They come to the Temple everyday and seem delighted to learn all about me. They act like a righteous nation that would never abandon the laws of God. They ask me to take action on their behalf, pretending they want to be near me. 3) We have fasted before you! they say. "Why aren't you impressed? We have been very hard on ourselves, and you don't even notice it!" "I will tell you why!" I respond. "It's because you are fasting to please yourselves. Even while you fast, you keep oppressing your workers. 4) What good is fasting when you keep on fighting and quarreling? This kind of fasting will never get you anywhere with me. 5) you humble yourselves by going through the motions of penance, bowing your heads like reeds bending in the wind. You dress in burlap and cover yourselves with ashes. Is this what you call fasting? Do you really think this will please the Lord? 6) "No, this is the kind of fasting I want: Free those who are wrongly imprisoned; lighten the burden of those who work for you. Let the oppressed go free, and remove the chains that bind people. 7) Share your food with the hungry, and give shelter to the homeless. Give clothes to those who need them, and not hide from relatives who need your help. 8) "Then your salvation will come like the dawn, and your wounds will quickly heal.

Your godliness will lead you forward, and the glory of the Lord will protect you from behind. 9) Then when you call, the Lord will answer. 'Yes, I am here,' He will quickly reply, "Remove the yoke of oppression. Stop pointing your finger and spreading vicious rumors! 10) Feed the hungry, and help those in trouble. Then your light will shine out from the darkness, and the darkness around you will be as bright as noon." 11) The Lord will guide you continually, giving you water when you are dry and restoring your strength. You will be like a well-watered garden, like an ever-flowing spring."

Would you believe that Abraham Lincoln prayed and fasted? God's spirit directed his steps. Not only did he fast, but lead others in both houses of congress and in our nation to join him. Not many know about this true worship and seeking of God that caused the glory of the Lord to protect President Lincoln and the nation from behind. It is however recorded in history and we continually give God the glory for a day of prayer continues to be honored yearly in our nation.

I'm determined to live the rest of my life serving God. If that means fasting as I pray, I definitely want to do it in a manner that pleases Him. Jesus had this to say as He taught about fasting in Matthew 6:16-18,

"And when you fast don't make it

obvious, as the hypocrites do, for they try to look miserable and disheveled so people will admire them for their fasting. I tell you the truth that is the only reward they will ever get. 17) But when you fast, comb your hair and wash your face. 18) Then no one will notice that you are fasting, except your Father, who knows what you do in private. And your Father, who sees everything, will reward you."

Having God's presence in my life is mind-blowing in itself. Benefits and rewards come through Him and His glory will protect you from behind. Yup! This is truly one of my greatest lessons about the glory of the Lord and I am giving Him the glory for it. You can believe that!!! My being alive and having this avenue of sharing my faith with you is testimony alone, in my opinion, that He had plans for me far greater than I ever realized. It is written in Jeremiah 29:11,

"For I know the plans I have for you," says the Lord. "They are plans for good and not for disaster, to give you a future and a hope."

This one Scripture verse helps us to know how God feels about us and thinks about us. He doesn't change! The truth and hope I've found in these words are for anyone who puts their trust in the Lord wholeheartedly.

Chapter Nine

We give God the glory throughout our lives in a number of different ways. We belong to the One who created us and we have been given the breath of life. We use this breath to praise God! You can even hear this breath leave our mouths as we shout "Hallelujah!" We could not give breath if it had not first been given to us. Neither can we give glory to God if we had not been *given it by Him. In John 17:20-24 Jesus speaks of glory being given to believers as He prays to the Father:* 22)

"I have given them the glory you gave me so they may be as one as we are one. 23) I am in them and you are in me. May they experience such perfect unity that the world will know that you sent me and that you love them as much as you love me. 24) Father I want these whom you have given me to be with me where I am. Then they can see all the glory you gave me because you loved me even before the world began!"

Jesus also put emphasis on the glory our Father had

given Him before the world began. This is talking about a place where we go after our lives on earth are over. Glory is something you can see! Jesus prayed that these that were given to Him would be with Him where He is. Then they can see all the glory the Father gave Him because He loved Jesus even before the world began!

Through faith in the Son of God we have glory and give our Father the glory that we have acquired. Jesus gave us the glory that He was given so that we may be one as He and the Father are one. He wants us to experience such perfect unity that the world will know that He was sent by God and that God loves us as much as He loves His Son Jesus.   Isn't that awesome? God loves us as much as He loves Jesus!

Over these years I've gotten so much encouragement to keep reading God's word, studying it, believing on it and being obedient to it. A letter my mother wrote me on this stationary has a picture of President Barak Obama at the top and the words "Repentance Brings Change" under it. I want to share what she sent to me back in March 2013: "My Beloved Son. To God be the glory for the great things He has done. He gave His only Son! His Son Jesus gave His life because we owed a debt we could not pay. He paid that debt on that old rugged cross. He suffered and died but He didn't stay in the grave. He's alive! And has all power in His hand. His *resurrection power abides in us. Al-le-lu-ia! Praise God Almighty." That's what my beloved mother wrote me.*

Chapter Ten

*From suffering to glory
1Peter 4:14b
(NKJV)"…..Blessed are you, for the <u>Spirit of glory</u> and of God rests upon you."*

Whenever anyone asked me how I'm doing, I usually respond with, "Blessed and highly favored." That's a known expression of faith in the Christian community. Whether I'm experiencing hardship or having moments of joy and great peace, I will generally answer the same way. If not with a smile on my face I'll have a smile in my eyes! It's been hard to suffer for my sins but it's a privilege for me to suffer for being a Christian. 1Peter 4:12-16 makes what I'm saying plain and very clear.

12) "Dear friends, don't be surprised at the fiery trials you are going through, as if something strange were happening to you. 13) Instead, be very glad- for these trials make you partners with Christ in His suffering, so that you will have the wonderful joy of seeing His glory when it is revealed to all the world.

14) So be happy when you are insulted for being a Christian, for then the glorious Spirit of God rests upon you. 15) If you suffer, however, it must not be for murder, stealing, making trouble or prying into other people's affairs. 16) But it is no shame to suffer for being a Christian. Praise God for the privilege of being called by His name!"

This praise that we give to God in our suffering is pleasing to Him. We give Him the glory when we understand what His will is for us. His will is clearly expressed in these Scriptures. Jesus suffered greatly for our sins until He was killed on the cross. The death penalty was imposed upon Jesus and we read about Him being blameless, without guilt and actually found to be innocent by Pontius Pilate the Roman governor and also by King Herod in Luke 23:13-15.

I surely suffer for my crimes by being in solitary confinement with the death penalty as my sentence. This isn't the kind of suffering that causes me to have the Spirit of glory and of God resting upon me. It's when I'm persecuted because of my faith in Christ Jesus in any way. My even talking about Jesus sometimes causes others to separate from me. Here in prison the popular conversations center around sports, how much money or canteen you have, how often people visit you, telephone use or how you can hold up in a fight or size up to other prisoners. Talking about the Holy Scriptures is a far cry from what we consider to be politically correct conversation. Following the teachings of Christ will cause a man to be looked upon as weak in this environment. But time and time again believers and non-believers alike have told me that I'm a better man than they are after someone has cussed me out and I did not respond in kind or like manner. Honestly I will tell you that I've been cussed out or called ugly names because of something I've said or done. I've also been treated badly and was not to blame. No matter, I set out to practice blessing those who curse me, doing good and praying for those who have used me spitefully. I've not returned evil behavior for evil behavior that came my way. At these times and as a follower of the Lord Jesus Christ, I know that the Spirit of glory and God rest upon me. So even in this place of earthly punishment, I suffer for Christ sake, but God instructs all of His children *to trust that He is with us through it all. 1Peter 4:19 says:*

"So if you are suffering in a manner that pleases God, keep on doing what is right, and trust your lives to the God who created you, for He will never fail you."

I am blessed to suffer being a Christian, a child of God and an heir in the household of a loving Father. I want you to understand that I am not speaking of my suffering as a convicted felon. It is written in 1Peter 4:15:

"If you suffer, however, it must not

be for murder, stealing, making trouble or prying into other people's affairs."

God's word clearly teaches us exactly what kind of suffering causes the Spirit of glory and of God to rest upon a person. Isn't that wonderful? Be encouraged by these verses in Romans 8:14-17

"For all who are led by the Spirit of God are children of God. 15) So you have not received a spirit that makes you fearful slaves. Instead, you received God's spirit when He adopted you as His own children. Now we call Him, "Abba, Father." 16) For His Spirit joins with our spirit to affirm that we are God's children. 17) And since we are His children, we are His heirs. In fact, together with Christ we are heirs of God's glory. But if we are to share His glory, we must also share His suffering."

The oldest man currently on South Carolina death row, told me more than once, about the hardships he faced while living as a believer and sharing that faith with others here in prison. I'll never forget the look on his face as he warned me to be careful. Another man a little older than myself, has a calling to preach the Gospel, shared his fears with me. He said that if I go on the prison yard with that "Jesus, Jesus mess, I'll get my head busted open." God's word tells us this in 1 Timothy 4:12,

"Yes, and everyone who wants to live a godly life in Christ Jesus will suffer persecution."

Glory be to God our Father and Saviour Jesus Christ for counting me worthy to suffer as one of His children and not merely as a prisoner on death row. Thank God that He uses the foolish to confound the wise. Thank Him for using me in a weak position in life to win those who are strong in this life. I'm fully convinced that He will have mercy and compassion on whoever He chooses. God knows I do not deserve it! He's allowing the Spirit of glory and of God to rest upon me and I'm certain as I can be that it's because He loves us all so, so, so very much. Can we all use whatever faith we currently have to all say, "Glory Be To God!?"

Conclusion

It's been my privilege to share these few things with you about the glory that we've been given, simply so we can give it all back to the One who is truly worthy of all the glory, honor and praise. Pray for my spiritual growth. I'll be praying for yours. In our bodies which is the temple of the Holy Spirit we say, **Glory!**

Made in the USA
Columbia, SC
15 September 2024